HAY THERE!

written by **J.R. Francis**
illustrated by **Elena Harman**

TO MY PARENTS AND GRANDPARENTS

who taught me the value of hard work and
who continue to show me their love and support
both here and from above

When John was young and it was fall, he'd hear his father say, "Coming up one Saturday, we'll have to haul the hay."

Seed had been planted in the spring
And watered with great care,
And pretty soon the hay would look
Like long, green, growing hair.

And little John would think and wait
And worry day-to-day,
Because you know, it's hard and not too fun
To have to haul the hay.

But the tractor drove around the field
And seemed to have a tail,
And out the other end would come
A nicely packed hay bale.

And once the bales were all up there
And stacked so very high,
John climbed on top and it did seem
He could almost touch the sky.

He'd ride the bales through street and lane
And take them to the barn,
And then the bales would take a ride
Up where they'd stay so warm.

And when the cows could eat and eat
And grow a little fatter,
Just then John knew that his hard work
Had really, really mattered!

He was happy to help the cows
He knew and loved so dear,
And he'd be ready to haul more hay
In the next upcoming year.

© 2020 J.R. Francis

IN MEMORY OF THE YORK/FRANCIS FARM
Springville, Utah, USA

Milton Keynes UK
Ingram Content Group UK Ltd.
UKHW051818050124
435541UK00004B/137